The Making of Budworm Farm

Andrea Suarez Hill

Goose River Press
Waldoboro, Maine

Copyright © 2020 Andrea Suarez Hill.

All rights reserved. No part of this book may be reproduced in any form without written permission from the publisher, except by a reviewer who may quote brief passages in a review to be printed in a newspaper or magazine.

Library of Congress Card Number: 2020930067

ISBN: 978-1-59713-211-4

First Printing, 2020

Photos Credits:
Front cover photo by Megan Cogswell
Back cover photo by Andrea Suarez Hill
Dedication and "Smithy" photos by Ian A. Hill
"Lesson" photo by Arthur Hill
    (Horse: Ain't Misbehavin', Paula Foote, owner.)
"Mares' Day," "Equus," and "Roy"& bio photos
    by Megan Cogswell
All other photos by Andrea Suarez Hill

Published by
Goose River Press
3400 Friendship Road
Waldoboro ME 04572
e-mail: gooseriverpress@roadrunner.com
www.gooseriverpress.com

This book is dedicated to

Arthur Hill, my best friend, and all the creatures of

Budworm Farm.

CONTENTS

Seeds

Seed//1
Hallowed//2
Reflection//3
Angst//4
Moon Spinner//5
Dream Catcher//6
The Boxer//7
Crash//8
Pictures//9
Home//10

Seasons

Seasons//13
Summer Current//14
Beach Day//15
July//16
Sea Change//17
September//19
Gratitude//20
One Last Decembral Day//22
Boreas//23
March//24
Hope//25
Monday//26

CONTENTS

Equus

Smithy//29
Passage//31
Trafficked//33
Night Check//35
Gone//37
Mares' Day//40
Alone//41
Savvy//42
Equus//44

Wildlife

Qigong//47
Yearlings//48
Call Me Harmony//49
Ravens//51
Raptor//53
Low Tide//54
Post Paris//55

Mentors

Roy//59
A Calling//60
Victor//61
Ginny//63
Lesson//65

Acknowledgments

Friends and family have bestowed on me encouragement, insight and support:

Fred Lowe, a poet's poet who designed and helped to organize this book; Peggy Grubel, Sherry Rier, Jackie Lowe, Jenny Spencer, Valerie Lawson of the Great Wass Women's Writers' Group and Bunny Richards of Trescott; Jerry George who guided me into a world of publishers; Melanie Fergerson at Fundy Bay Printing whose help over the years has put my poetry in print; my brother, Tony Suarez and his wife, Laurel, whose presence is steadfast; my mother, Thea Alderman, who gave me the gift of life.

My thanks and my love.

Forward

In 1985, my husband, Arthur, and I were going to call our eleven acres of forest in Jonesboro, Maine "The Lough" due to its location on a bay at the mouth of the Chandler River about a half mile from the ocean. But, as we worked to clear the land, a friend who helped us, Jon Watts, said "you have a budworm farm" and the name stuck. Budworm Farm was born and stands today because of townspeople like Jon, Mark Alley, Al Caruso, Ginny Fieldman, the Snowdeal Family and Mary & Eddie Stubbs.

Arthur and I met in New York City. He was an actor and I was a picture editor for Time, Incorporated. He told me, "I was a farrier in California," after we spoke about our love of horses. But our equine passions slept until we moved to Maine and bought an unbroken Arab cross. We called him "Brumbie" after the horses made famous in "The Man from Snowy River" film. Our life together with horses began as we made a farm to fit our vision. Weather, wildlife, family and friends all played a part. These poems express the life we've made together over the past 34 years.

~ 1 ~
SEEDS

Seed

The aperture insists on focus,
                dwells on what's undone.
But a mind's eye moves
                as wind on water.
Images like waves collapse
                one by one:
time-released exposure
                makes a collage,
present become the past.
                A picture unfolds,
all years superimposed,
                single but whole,
an embryo.

Hallowed

A black wood stove gone gray with white heat,
   claw marks of buried dogs on worn pine floor,
impressions of first words written on a cherry desk,
   obits stuck in decayed books like prayer cards in purse
   pockets
with a crinkled image of a colt bred, grown and gone
   with hoof beats that echoed in the pasture:

Each a knot tied in the heart that slows its sap's flow
   like a fence reframes movement of a once wild life
forced to travel trapped by borders
   cut by seasons after the summery sun falls
and sends shadow farther down the hill
   until All Hallows when dead walk unfrayed,
again golden amid green days.

Reflection

My mirror is heavy,
                a hand-held god in control.
It holds a woman
                and a girl who rides a unicorn,
but can't make them whole.
                Amid their years,
a likeness flickers from the glass,
                taps her heart and says
"it's in here"
        as if she were a book
about instinct, fate and
                a life's weight.

I hold it before me
                and a choice is made:
the small giant within
                breaks her silver legacy,
smiles and makes from
                its crystal shards
a nimbus to wear
                through time's eclipse,
no longer a servant
                who lives to please
a reflection separate
                from her soul.

Angst

On her unmade bed,
she worries splinters
worked into fingers
from firewood...

Red pus-filled bumps
burst as tears,
wits race to rest,
panic waits...

Books sit, pages unturned.
Poised to work
with pen and paper
she clings to a pencil ledge...

Cracked nails chewed,
words fail, mind spasms and
reinless prayers ride
with Morai

Moon Spinner

From the river's bed
                a moon sated and
silver crawls over the flats,
                    meets lead-red mud,
moves my horizon,
              reshapes the shore,
unseats mauve skies and
                  slate grey clouds
above a drain tide
            as a poem lets loose
with a pull words work
                on gravity channeled
through an inner sea.

Dreamcatcher

Thick as heavy cream,
fog hugged the sun
above the bay, tight
as the armor of night
held close a dreamer...

dressed to kill critics,
a harem of hypocrites,
formed long black lines,
a gauntlet of double edged
cold comments so sharp
each cut a plank in reason...

'She felt a funeral in her brain,'
the barbed words chosen
to cut bone, but
flags blown to bright bits,
prayers pinned to a line,
cut mourning's damp doom...

and a new moon rode
low over the dream's cape,
a narrow blade
that cut the string
between night and day.

The Boxer
For Joseph A. Suarez (1923-1994)

   Cool eyes watch moves and
wait for hubris to crack
    spewing ribbons of red down
temples, cheeks, chin and chest
    until sweat wet biceps gesture
no more to a vulturous crowd,
    his mythical family, friends, fans,
who flee a titleless frame,
    a beltless martyr.

Dollars demand streamlined sacrifices,
    a steel-tempered hero
always on offense even when
    battered to corners,
a matador gored
    on a blood-stained mat.
The battle ended
    with his trailing hand.

Weakened, openings wasted
    mano o mano on ruthless youth,
he was caught between instinct and art with
    gloved fists stilled but still clenched,
limbs collapsed and cramped
    below crossed hands shouting out.
Cameras chattered,
    arena lights arced and fell
like fallible stars.

Crash

For Ian A. Hill

The fix kicked in
as he lay wide-eyed
between sand and sky,
high, broad and wide,
the sea invisible,
an azure edge,
no Pacific sounds,
only his blood
pounding to leave
his skin behind
beneath a windshield
smashed to crystal web.

A shard sliced
the sailor's bicep and
a maroon dragon tattoo
bled mountains of myth
he could not claim
after the cobalt blue
Subaru collided with smack
and arranged a release
to soothe wounds
no one could reach.

Pictures

Green designs grow,
wait to be born,
upon blank pages
tissues form.

Intuition's celebration
springs from my pen,
a cradle creation
shaped to perceive.

Sensitive skin distilled,
it spills over
until freed,
a gift
fit to read.

Home

Our house wears weather
on a shingled face.
Once buff cedar shakes are
curled and gray.

Each speaks sun, rain,
ice or snow:
ridged, rolled edges,
some split in two,
they know life inside
mirrors them, too.

Not sorry, not scared,
both sides know
age spares nothing
not shared.

~ 2 ~
SEASONS

Seasons

Since long since
   beneath fake Tiffany shade,
Grandfather's clock chimes
   and binds calendar days
when words can't be trusted...

summer lays slippery on iced
   white porch with peels of paint,
manure pile smokes
   a scent like Dad's tobacco and
cold seeps into calloused hands...

another dawn sparks dark
   frosty bay silver as
the moon sinks itself and
   sets west in undressed maples
with my dreams half grown...

in me this movement I see:
   Luna fades to day,
leaves dooryard and beyond
   blue as twilight in morning,
her ripe yellow moment past.

Summer Current

In your absence I float
atop a bay of memory,
a faceless, salt-stained and
pallid cheeked island...

a childlike land still
needing to be rocked
by the rhythmic lap
of a well-summered sea...

but the too tidal and
unquiet wave you are
won't allow me calm repose
in the muscled grasp of
two strange peninsulas.

Beach Day

Waves' white water
gift grey after grey
sea to beach,
manes and tails
above Earth's reach.

Comber after comber,
salt air rings with
hooves in harmony,
muscles flexed, sinews stretched,
carved and blessed.

Each breaker borne equus
roils with joy whilst
from ocean to sand
broad backs swing
and reins go slack.

July

A Full Buck Moon
        snorts contempt
at a cold front that
        opens summer's front door,
steps inside
        with wet, moonless boots
and stands to roar.
        A ruck with rain
spits through screens,
        heat scorches his sky,
flame on slate:
        horses bolt, dogs bark,
dories struggle to float.
        But the tide leaves
before morning sways
        over bay and
steams luminescent
        from cove to cove,
silent
    until heron wings
say "away"
        stroke for stroke
as fishermen row
        out to their boats.

Sea Change

Fish-heavy boats
plow down the reach
reeking bait and diesel.
Black-backed gulls arc
high to dive at scraps.
Sun-coated seals snooze
on hump-back stone, and
ocean swells sprawl over
mammoth storm worn walls.

A 9.9 Mercury hums a mantra
from Amesbury transom and,
deft as green crabs, we hop over
splintered dock pilings, hitch our skiff
to raid a private island. We pirates
jump a faded "No Trespass" sign,
race a falling tide
over broken boardwalk
to an unmanned light.

Hand-wrought door hinges and
a handle keepers once touched
on moss-covered brick and mortar open.
A spiral rust-stained staircase
leads to Stone Age tech that
once flashed its own code in crystal
and sounded a horn
sailors sought and obeyed.
We high-five the view.

September

"I am one acquainted with the night,"
      run against darkness
    as my mind recalls June
        in lemon light.
Every moment mattered.
 Our play
      added
           minutes
                each
                    day
before summer ceased,
  left your stall
         without
              your
                  call.
No white horse
        stands
            to bathe
                in moonshine.
The paddock's bare
        with
           blighted
                light,
no sound of
      silver
        shoes
           on
           printless
           ground.
I stare at air.

Gratitude

November gale whips
inlet water white.
On eel grass geese harbor
'til storm retreats, their
creamy breasts like boats beached.

Parched snow coats
birch and fir trees
where iridescent ravens
await my Thanksgiving feed.
Rumps to wind,
horse and does paw
for snowfield's green
as an eight-point buck
snorts and sniffs unfazed
while I deliver hay.

Red fox scurry up the drive,
in pine tree turkeys hide.
A feral cat friend
arcs over barn door,
home at last
as gusts force
gray juncos to grass
a beige plow scores.

Forest stewards all,
they welcome me outside,
a misfit toy
in Nature's sketch
who must aid
a planet on the edge.

One Last Decembral Day

Silence roars at dawn
over iced flats
as high tide skates
on crusty mud and
mute gulls mingle with chimney smoke.
Bare hands and fingers burn,
trees snap, cracked boots creak.
Along a tree-lined ridge
firs felled by salt from
new moon overflows
sleep in fall's washouts.
Their root wads reach
like crippled feet.

Sun's grey ghost
slips above a tidal basin.
Stalled fog, frozen dust,
paints opaque equine shapes
in cotton light.
White shadows stir and
nicker for first feed.
A buried voice speaks
its tears behind eyes and throat,
wets my cheeks and
begs this peace bide another year.

Boreas

The purple winged north god
               sweeps through spruce.
His song cuts flesh,
               breath pierces chimes,
dusts snow over home,
               it sparkles and groans.

Moonlight lays
             her quilt down,
bright white.
               She glides across
a shared bed
             in passage west.

In night's womb
               Eos stretches
horizon's seam,
               draws out rose light.
Eyes open
          on dappled, crimson sea.

Dressed for dawn,
               this goddess directs
her Titan son
             to sing up Spring
and this day
             to bless.

March

March seventh, minus seven,
sea smoke white-washes sun,
a ghost afloat ice
near break up in bay.
Boats, gulls, ducks doze,
minutes morph to months,
my mood slumps...

mailboxes decorate dirt roads
with fences plowed down,
saline sandstorms blind drivers
on broken, bumpy black top,
road signs peek from snow banks
like green shoots,
red squirrels run when fox pounce...

fisher cats meow in moonlight,
deer chew cedar trees
low with snow,
ravens' beaks pick and shovel
communal crumbs
and dent a glacial crown
over sleepy, supple soil.

Hope

The moon rolls over, shrugs and shrinks beneath the sun's weight on ice-calloused snow that glares at an iris blue sky.

Glazed mud flats pocked with rocks gleam at low tide while frosted streams seep and meander to a rimed shoreline.

In an iceless bay, middle ground rises surrounded by silver floes clinging to sand soon to float on open ocean.

A gust off the water slaps my back, fills a bucket and spills morning oats while Seamus nickers and stomps.

His black nostrils blow white steam to winds before he tastes kernels like bread baked and broken for Mass.

A rusted shovel scrapes crystalled manure, grinds against earth, echoes loud in the voiceless dawn...deer disappear, mere thoughts without words.

Cracked, chapped hands cut a bale's twine to free fresh-cut hay fields from flakes I shake as
Helios and his steeds rise higher each day.

Monday

March wind spins dead leaves,
spruce trees sound their whistle
to a steel gray sky that
hangs its girders low,
smothers sun's rise,
blackens bay's green glass
under cumulous pillows,
weightless, snowy shades
that billow, unfold and bend,
Nature's nurse who
asks her patient,
man-worn poor,
to rise once more.

~ 3 ~
EQUUS

Smithy

For Arthur E. Hill

Fire's out, forge decayed
    coal and iron spent,
shop's song silent,
    tires and tarps
press out old days
    and horses who'd wait
for farrier to fettle
    their feathered feet.
But fired and proved,
    his Peter Wright Patent
solid wrought anvil rests
    still on an oak stump
cut off winter's wood.
    Vertical grain inspired
a spring and ring,
    its own centurion hymn:
the swayed face,
    chisel edges chipped,
horn and heel pocked
    by hammer strikes
on shoes our horses wore
    level with toes rolled fair.

Learned in all skills
    known to smithies past,
he flowered in iron,
    bent steel to be

in flat open furnace,
    air forced through coal
orange hot in fire pot.
    Scarred leather chaps flapped
betwixt horse and hearth,
    each hoof nipped, measured, fit:
tools' echoed a rhythmic clang,
    embers glowed with bar stock
cut on hardy sharp,
    a shower of sparks,
blow by blow;
    steel bent, pritchel punched,
heels filed smooth
    and water cooled.
A strong, deft touch
    drove every nail point true,
straight side out,
    into a living wall;
clinched, rasped, dressed
    silver slippers made one by one,
his work now done.

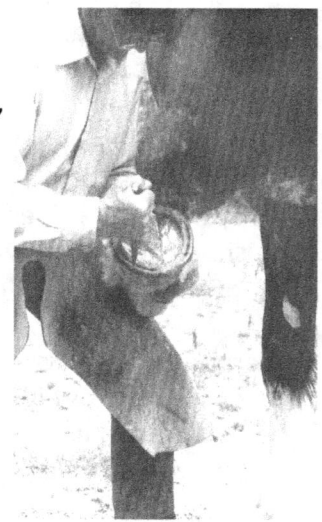

Passage

For Lee Bustard

The title page of summer always opened to
    Lee standing like Mercator's titan
atop a flatbed truck with
    five hundred bales framed by
the weight of light blue,
    sky he held with the sun
on his shoulders, a tank top
    showing his farmer's tan.
From his paws like rough sawn boards
    flew each fifty pounds of fodder
while we ground crew scattered and hopped
    quick to sweat as chaff filled floor and shirt.

Good hay turned the heavens
    on their axis until he stumbled
and broke his.
    Now beneath white light, Atlas endures in
frosted glass quarters full of quiet noise,
    the blunt poetry of I.C.U.
punctuated by ventilator pings, whispers,
    paper shuffled, the swish of yellow gowns
and rubber soles like the soft sound
    his footsteps made on last Fall's hunting ground.

A monitor's metallic eyes replaced deer in his sights,
    and jagged green lines on a screen track blood and being.
Around the family farm house
    tractor, tedder, and baler waited since fields were high
but he never again will bind with rough twine
    well dried grass stuffed tight morning 'til night.
The machines were brokered to highest bidders
    with the F 250 and a used RV.
Alone, the side-by-side swings in wind
    filled with fallen yellow leaf.

Trafficked

Pain wasn't new to him.
Proud flesh necklaced a heel.
A white scar adorned his spine.
His kick, shy and recoil
from a horseman's hand or
farrier's need to lift a hoof,
spoke of silent tactile terror then
a caller drawled his name, BB.

The two letter key turned tumblers
to a beaten prisoner's secret cell.
Snubbed securely to insecurity
against a barn wall with
cable tie down or head set rope,
his sinew and bone were winched
to fit a human failure's fantasies.

He stood invisible and waiting
in a windowless space
full of empty buckets,
breathing in short gasps
the stench of piss, manure and
dried sweat caked on an ebony coat
in crusty grey designs around
boiled up welts on
ribbed-filled skin.

Twitching at a sneeze, brush touch or
tack too quickly set,
gravity pulled him
through a new gate with
posts cemented like a vow
to heal his hobbled heart
and soften eyes on guard
with hands that cradle grief
and fingers like voices
that sing to mind and muscle.
His body keeps score.

Night Check

Back door to barn
winter shadows
redesign the dark.
Nickers sound
guttural equine requests
inside a squeaky gate,
blending silence with
duck lyrics in icy bay.

Flared nostrils wide as
doe eyes shine in
night light's silver streak
beneath a black forelock,
and fur-filled ears.
Their orchid shapes bow and
feed on loosened flakes,
sweet with summer's breath,
beside a warm bucket
poured and rising,
stalled sea smoke.

Our breaths evaporate,
his head warms my hands
tracing fine bones,
eyes, cheeks and jowl while
arms surround his neck
in mortal hug as
fingers comb ragged mane
and my nose burrows
in coat's bouquet,
perfumed with salt and hay.

A bay muzzle searches
pockets, seams worn gray
with catlike rubs
to scratch thick coat,
frosted lashes, whiskers and
snow smooth mouth.
Treats found and gifted,
our good night.

Gone

Strong, straight white washed fences,
figures who knew their ground,
protected their creatures and fell
forward together with posts
leaning toward each other
like old couples walk,
their boards gray and moss covered,
shrunken past middle age and
scores of frosts.

Sunk in dung,
a couch to rest upon,
the manure spreader spreads,
her wheels below
a steaming coverlet when once
she enjoyed greening fields
into summer forage with
an '86 Ford,
its primer passed to rust,
a doorless, floorless frame,
hollow as the hay loft
they once filled.

A barn sags on a cracked sill
like an elder creaky and
crooked on his cane.

(continued)

The roof is swayed
as the horses' backs
who cruise pastures out of work
waiting for a curry.
Its rafters are broken ribs that
protrude like hips that groan when
winds blow cold and
the loft struggles to hold
a chaff and seed load.

Inside a tack room rots.
Tired boots, unpolished aged soldiers
from horse shows past,
ankles broken, toes curled,
stand huddled beneath
bridles hung from pegs,
bits crusty with saliva,
leather reins stiff as
the last rider's hands.
Ribbons red, yellow, blue,
two walls full, stretch above
hard leather halters with
brass name plates rusted green,
hung in homage to
those gone away before
cobwebs caught whinnies
echoed in empty stalls,
calling through a farm bowed
to years gone 'round.

Mare's Day
For Ultimata (1991–2014)

"Tell me kemosabe
how one hundred horse years feel?
Do you still need to grab the reins
and run
using your magic
to find the power to kick on
or would you choose to rest
on soft straw to sooth your unruled soul ?"

"My hips shout out loud,
bone on bone,
every stride says stop.
We both wear our thick black coats
long into Spring and
have folds and pleats where muscles have been,
but let's hear once more
my hooves on the wind."

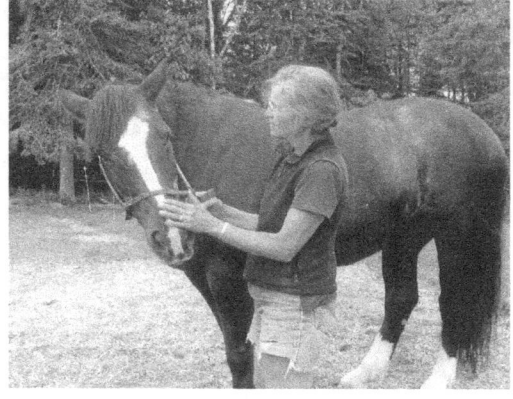

Alone

On a coltish May day
when wet green sod
flew behind his gallop,
he stood and snorted at
a backhoe's yellow claw
in moist brown clay,
coffin deep and waiting
to accept a centurion,
his unparalleled partner who
lay timeless beside it.

His whiskers twitched,
he nuzzled her grayed coat,
sniffed the black mane and
rhythmically rubbed his nose
over a hollow flank.
He nickered, nostrils quivered,
ears pricked, called again,
but only a loon's cry
carried by chilled gusts off
blue gray bay returned the call.

Savvy

On a moonless evening and
    rain-slick road
the semi's metal skin shimmers
    with wrap around light,
orange, red and white
    blink, sparkle, flash,
turn inside out a hushed fall night.

His silver grey coat quivers,
    he snorts yet stands,
poised beside his shed,
    watches, listens, senses threat.
A lead shank snaps
    to a leather halter
on a half-ton flight risk and
    his wood gate's unlatched.

As the turbo diesel clatters,
    a partnership resounds
"Walk on Roy" and
    left, right, left, right
horse and owner step toward
    dual high beams, blinkers and noise.
At the gangway to a bedded box,
    eyes and nostrils wide, he stops.

Though born to flee,
    four legs like rooted oaks plant.
He breathes deep, paws, poops, recovers and
    we march up side by side,
a rite of passage presides:
    Vaquero and driver, Jorge,
closes stall door, says "sabe"
    and tips his hat.

Equus

Horses are poems
                to feed, water, grow, train,
secret sharers living in my heart,
                        they're keepers of the
flame
who seek a massage, curry or brush
                before manure's taken as
words cut from a page
                or stones picked from feet,
those thoughts that hang incomplete.

A shedding blade like a pen
                    can find summer-sleek shine
in brevity that shapes stanzas' lines.
            Though ticklish spots are scratched,
one pleased too soon
            finds flaws arise,
a drama unfulfilled that
            holds fire and sorrow.

~ 4 ~
WILDLIFE

Qigong

White cheeked geese,
black legs barely bent,
honk and sweep over
a flat green fir land
in wedge formation
their feathered arms
holding the air
to land
weightless on water
with energy that floats
from beaks to web feet.
Complete.

yearlings

grey bamboo bones
        blend
              into last year's grass,
ebony eyes
      meet man and
             white flags fly as
birch-paper skins
      unfurl and
           flutter in March wind...
they flee
    finch-light
        on lithe green shoots,
fleet as arrows
      freed to the air
           both wear...

flora-fauna symmetry

Call Me Harmony

A baleen, number 3115
born in '01, last seen 2016.
My facial callosities,
a Celtic cross design,
passed down family tree
from mother, number 1815.

We surface swim slow
each spring from Florida
past Fundy to Gaspe,
St. Lawrence Gulf and Chaleur Bay.
Copepod rich, colder water
strains through my mouth,
good feed for calf and me.

Tankers and container ships
in our new summer home,
propellers, nets, lines, buoys
flood this sea room:
no spout, no broach, no fluke flung out,
its leading edge flayed by lines that
tangle about head, neck, mouth
and bind flippers to my sides.

On skin once coal black
white lesions grow with disease and stress.
Vessels strike and storm petrels peck
for lice on my mangled carcass
with orange welts, open wounds worse than
strikes from hand hurled harpoons.
I no longer struggle or call, months pass,
too weak to eat or swim,
my blubber floats for man to haul.

Ravens

March messengers, omens that call,
    black feathered merchants of change
who wait and watch,
    sweep through spruce canyons,
swoop so low
    air beneath wings vibrates and flows.
They know we aren't who we were,
    but will we, without knowing,
not know who we are?

Once we were taut and tan,
    undressed but for sunlight,
skinny-dipping in youth's waterfall
    beside a spring-fed lake,
chest to breast, lip to lip, holding fast,
    rolling dry in green high grass or
skipping through winter white water
    on seaweed and snow-dotted beach,
powering our songs with wine
    over the wind's buoy and waves' crash.

Our rag and bone shops gathered force,
    we toiled years with visions for a forest,
a salt water farm with mews was born.
    But now the farrier's hearth burns low,
his hammer beats on steel so slow.
    Corbies hear the hollow chime and know
the truth their prophecy divines.

Raptor

Ice goes to ground,
Persephone greens pastures,
beaks pierce earth,
all flocks feed.
Iridescent purple starlings
fan, whistle and wheel
across sun's cradle.
The speckled regiment
opens and closes its ranks as
a winged warrior,
who lurks alone,
glides and dives,
wings beat,
feathers explode and
a song dies.

Low Tide

Above over-buoyed bays that abide,
  few birds on the wing that once could
sing a hundred thousand strong,
  in sync with forage fish and
fed by full digestion on
  an Earth that supplied itself
with plenty for all migrations:

Arctic terns, eiders, plovers and
  sandpipers search for food
to fuel themselves
  before Fall's cool. They stay
longer but take forced flight
  underweight and unable to roost
with water too high to rest.

Under a sky like sand
  riffled by waves,
birds land on Down East seas,
  destinations ordained but
designs disturbed by draggers,
  erosion, and a broken climate,
spilling death on barren shores.

Post Paris

Nature hates walls
                and fences with
borders to manage,
                  flora, fauna and
migrants to crush as
                    Man profits,
poaches and poisons,
                    unsatisfied
by his design
          to separate space
by red line:
        forests, plains, peaks,
sea and sky die
             while he whistles
earth's grave grows wide:
                    fire, flood, famine, disease,
epilogues each
          a pass to oblivion
in unison writ
            with killer unreason.

~ 5 ~
MENTORS

Roy

We riffle through the woods,
    pebbles tossed to a pond,
touch maple leaves and fir trees
    that filter sun streams
through our silver manes.
    I hum "Moon River" to
a white-tailed dapple grey
    with two hind socks and a blaze
on his doe-eyed, freckled face.

Over a sand and cedar bark dance floor,
    I stride toward his tail,
he yields hind legs,
    a two-step right then
forward I flow as he turns
    front feet with mine.
Every move of his hooves
    shapes our first season and
makes not a splash, but
    ripples that fuse
the dance we will choose.

A Calling
For Minor Rootes (1931-2017)

Harbor seals' dark eyes
   stare from sea
and granite perch...

An island's bell
   warned as waves
rose and fell...

Silken water lapped skiff,
   seaweed swayed its tresses
and over rocks cascaded...

Sky and ocean one,
   profiled by islands black,
a wall of grey horizon...

Over gunwale deep, dark
   clouds laid on the sun
and moved with tide's mark...

It swept off ashes white
   lightly spread by hand,
the beauty of a man...

Limits left, infinity found,
   his calling complete,
fired full and round.

Victor
For Victor Riesel (1913-1995)

I called, he spoke; I read, he wrote
   or stared at the plaster ceiling
piecing together secrets
   while his fingers tapped on his wood desk
in time to the teletype
   that spat out noisy news,
a yellow pile on faded linoleum floor.
   No security save his dark glasses
behind a frosted glass office door
   with solid black lettering;
he faced a window
   that opened on a brick wall.

Into whispering rooms
   his questions followed
government and union men
   through dark and twisted tunnels
as they scurried about.
   He painted in print daily
deeds done and undone
   in a crime web woven
so tight spiders
   caught themselves.

He shouted them
   out on his Olivetti,
replayed research from memory;
   He heard every side
from Gerald Ford to George Meany,
   his words formed a tapestry
before deadline
   when his fists often pounded
to help him see
   every lead and source,
fit them snug and
   framed his challenge
to those who feared his fire
   twenty years after acid
flew from Telvi's hand.
   My eyes were his.

Ginny
For Virginia Fieldman (1922–2014)

Glassy gray eyes stared
                at a sheetrock sky,
wilted lips moved
                with morphine's drip to
kill a threadbare heart
                in a five foot giant
too big to die,
                too weak to live when
timeless words from
                her featherweight voice
rode with her to eternity:
                "we're the luckiest people alive."

At her dirt simple dooryard service,
                pintos stood as if called
between weary barn and home,
                her light forever gone from
us across the river.
                Chill salt breezes stroked manes and
hair of a rowdy, reverent flock
                who echoed memories in praise
of her boisterous strength and
                endless chores her hands were
to deliver all creatures from
                lives tossed aside, broken, lost,
to her Eden far Down East.

Waist-high white weeds swayed,
                hooves tapped deep paths over
aged manure's smoked tobacco smell
                      one long, last summer:
The empty woodshed frowned,
                but a sitting room smiled with
photos, books, cards, and thanks
                  for free rooms "rented"
with her universal conscience
              that blazed our way and
the legend of Windrise Farm.

Lesson

I will carry you

with me as

one.

Hear my back,

hoof and heart

speak.

Feel what I say.

Forget self,

give.

Be generous with

hands, reins, reward.

Every

ride is a refuge,

within is without.

When you listen,

questions are answered.

Credits

From A Far Corner: An Anthology of Poetry from the Easternmost Reaches of Maine first published the following poems in 2018 "Crash," "Gone," "March," "Hallowed," "Dreamcatcher," and "Passage."

The Aurorean first published the following poems, "Moon Spinner" (2016), "Seasons" (2017), and "July" (2018).

A Living History of Northern and Downeast Maine: Harvest Recess and Picker Shacks first published "Ginny" in 2016.

Goose River Anthology, 2018, first published "Beach Day," "Monday," "Sea Change," and "Yearlings."

Goose River Anthology, 2019, first published "Gratitude" and "One Last Decembral Day."

The Binnacle first published "Low Tide" and "Smithy" in 2017.

3 Nations Anthology published "Smithy" in 2017.

I am grateful to these publications for permission to reprint.

Andrea Suarez Hill grew up in New England. She had a career in print, broadcast and photo-journalism in New York City until 1987 when she moved to Maine. She is a life-long horse woman who enjoys the outdoors on the salt water farm she and her husband, Arthur, created. Her poetry is inspired by the sea and all of nature that surrounds them. Together they spent years shoeing horses from Calais to Deer Isle. Clients became friends. A special way of life was found in the people and culture of Down East that influences all of her poetry. This book celebrates that journey.

Her work has been published in "the Aurorean," "3 Nations Anthology," "The Binnacle," "From A Far Corner: An Anthology of Poetry from the Easternmost Reaches of Maine," "Goose River Anthology," "A Living History of Northern and Downeast Maine: Harvest Recess and Picker Shacks," "The Sun Journal," "A Dangerous New World, Maine Voices on the Climate Crisis."

www.ingramcontent.com/pod-product-compliance
Lightning Source LLC
Chambersburg PA
CBHW052123070526
44586CB00016B/2054